NATURAL WONDERS
GRAND CANYON

by Katie Chanez

Ideas for Parents and Teachers

Pogo Books let children practice reading informational text while introducing them to nonfiction features such as headings, labels, sidebars, maps, and diagrams, as well as a table of contents, glossary, and index.

Carefully leveled text with a strong photo match offers early fluent readers the support they need to succeed.

Before Reading

- "Walk" through the book and point out the various nonfiction features. Ask the student what purpose each feature serves.
- Look at the glossary together. Read and discuss the words.

Read the Book

- Have the child read the book independently.
- Invite them to list questions that arise from reading.

After Reading

- Discuss the child's questions. Talk about how they might find answers to those questions.
- Prompt the child to think more. Ask: Did you know about the Grand Canyon before reading this book? What more would you like to learn about it?

Pogo Books are published by Jump!
5357 Penn Avenue South
Minneapolis, MN 55419
www.jumplibrary.com

Copyright © 2025 Jump!
International copyright reserved in all countries.
No part of this book may be reproduced in any form without written permission from the publisher.

Library of Congress Cataloging-in-Publication Data

Names: Chanez, Katie, author.
Title: Grand Canyon / by Katie Chanez.
Description: Minneapolis, MN: Jump!, Inc., [2025]
Series: Natural wonders | Includes index.
Audience: Ages 7-10
Identifiers: LCCN 2024028679 (print)
LCCN 2024028680 (ebook)
ISBN 9798892135375 (hardcover)
ISBN 9798892135382 (paperback)
ISBN 9798892135399 (ebook)
Subjects: LCSH: Grand Canyon (Ariz.) –Juvenile literature. | CYAC: Grand Canyon (Ariz.)
Classification: LCC F788 .C46 2025 (print)
LCC F788 (ebook)
DDC 979.132–dc23/eng/20240703
LC record available at https://lccn.loc.gov/2024028679
LC ebook record available at https://lccn.loc.gov/2024028680

Editor: Alyssa Sorenson
Designer: Molly Ballanger

Photo Credits: DimaSid/Shutterstock, cover; Mateas George Sebastian/Shutterstock, 1; Yongyut Kumsri/Shutterstock, 3; EpicStockMedia/Shutterstock, 4; DeSid/iStock, 5; James Marvin Phelps/Shutterstock, 6-7tl; K Hanley CHDPhoto/Shutterstock, 6-7tr; Jeff Colburn/iStock, 6-7bl; Fischer0182/Dreamstime, 6-7br; Ronald Karpilo/Alamy, 8; tobiasjo/iStock, 9; PannaPhoto/Shutterstock, 10-11; We Wander Everywhere/iStock, 12-13; AlbertoGonzalez/Shutterstock, 14-15; Michael Nolan/Robert Harding Picture Library/SuperStock, 16; Edward S. Curtis/Library of Congress, 17; Francisco Blanco/Shutterstock, 18-19tl; John M. Chase/iStock, 18-19tr; JeffGoulden/iStock, 18-19bl; Jim Mallouk/Shutterstock, 18-19br; miroslav_1/iStock, 20-21; travellight/Shutterstock, 23.

Printed in the United States of America at Corporate Graphics in North Mankato, Minnesota.

TABLE OF CONTENTS

CHAPTER 1
Rocky Canyon.. 4

CHAPTER 2
How It Formed... 8

CHAPTER 3
Life in the Canyon... 16

QUICK FACTS & TOOLS
At a Glance.. 22
Glossary... 23
Index... 24
To Learn More... 24

CHAPTER 1
ROCKY CANYON

The Colorado River flows through **steep**, rocky walls in Arizona. What is this place? It is the Grand **Canyon**.

Colorado River

It is the largest canyon in the United States. It stretches 278 miles (447 kilometers). It is 18 miles (29 km) across at its widest point. It is about one mile (1.6 km) deep!

CHAPTER 1   5

bighorn sheep

rattlesnake

mule deer

California condor

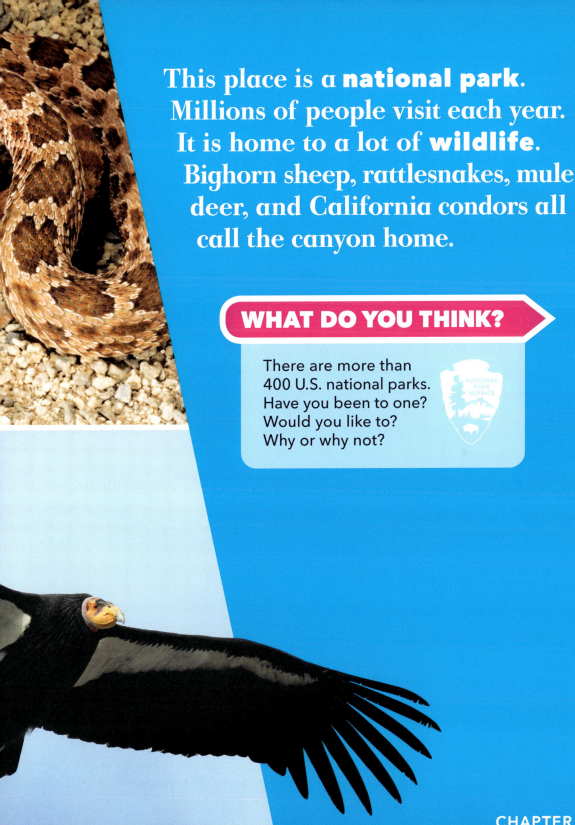

This place is a **national park**. Millions of people visit each year. It is home to a lot of **wildlife**. Bighorn sheep, rattlesnakes, mule deer, and California condors all call the canyon home.

WHAT DO YOU THINK?

There are more than 400 U.S. national parks. Have you been to one? Would you like to? Why or why not?

CHAPTER 1

CHAPTER 2
HOW IT FORMED

The Grand Canyon took millions of years to form. The oldest rocks are at the bottom. They are as old as North America! Scientists study the rocks. Each **layer** is from a different time. It tells us what Earth was like when it formed.

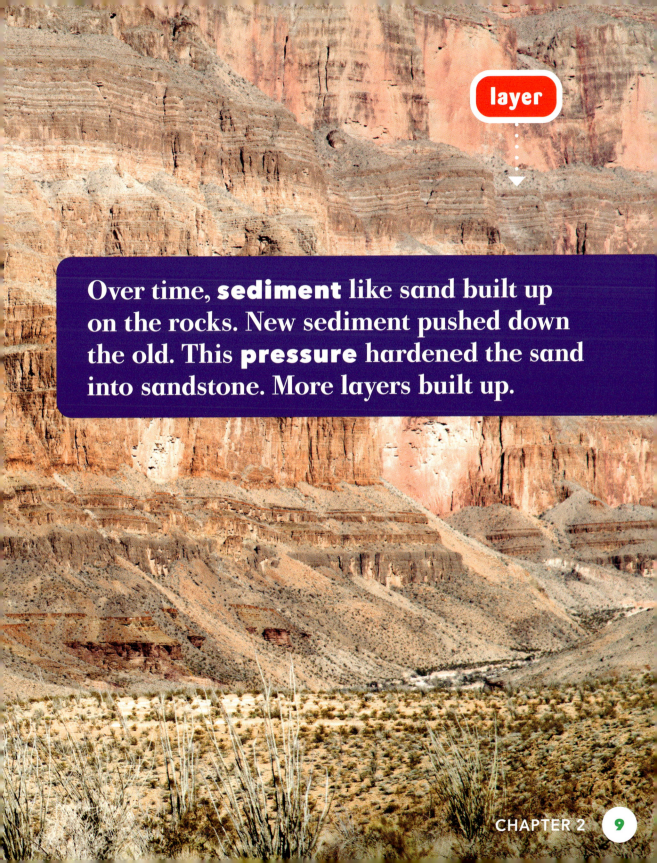

layer

Over time, **sediment** like sand built up on the rocks. New sediment pushed down the old. This **pressure** hardened the sand into sandstone. More layers built up.

CHAPTER 2

Earth is made of **tectonic plates**. They move very slowly. Between 70 and 50 million years ago, two plates pushed together. This pushed the land up. A **plateau** formed.

The Colorado River flows across the plateau. The water began to **erode** the rock. Over time, the river **carved** the canyon.

DID YOU KNOW?

The Grand Canyon is still changing. The Colorado River erodes one foot (0.3 meters) of rock every 200 years!

CHAPTER 2 · 13

Rain erodes the sides of the canyon. This makes it wider. Water also flows into cracks in the rock. When it gets cold, the water freezes. Ice takes up more space than water. It makes the cracks bigger. The rock breaks. It leaves the canyon wider.

TAKE A LOOK!

How did the Grand Canyon form? Take a look!

1 Sediment piled on rock. Some hardened into sandstone.

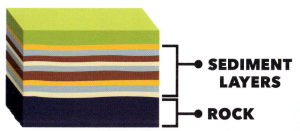

2 Tectonic plates pushed the land up. A plateau formed.

3 Water and weather eroded the rock.

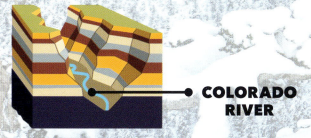

CHAPTER 2   15

CHAPTER 3
LIFE IN THE CANYON

People have lived in the Grand Canyon for about 10,000 years! The Ancestral Puebloan people started living here around 200 BCE. They left the area around 1100 CE. Visitors can still see **traces** of them today!

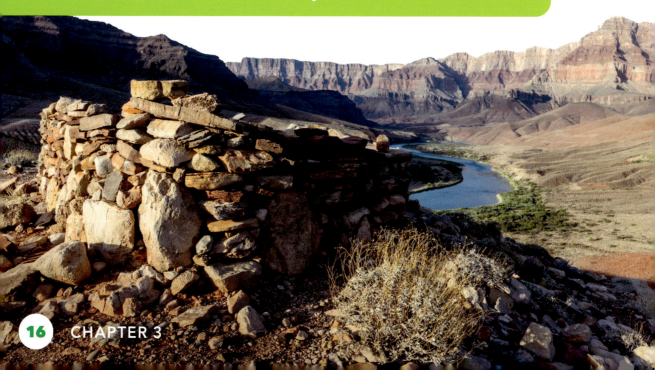

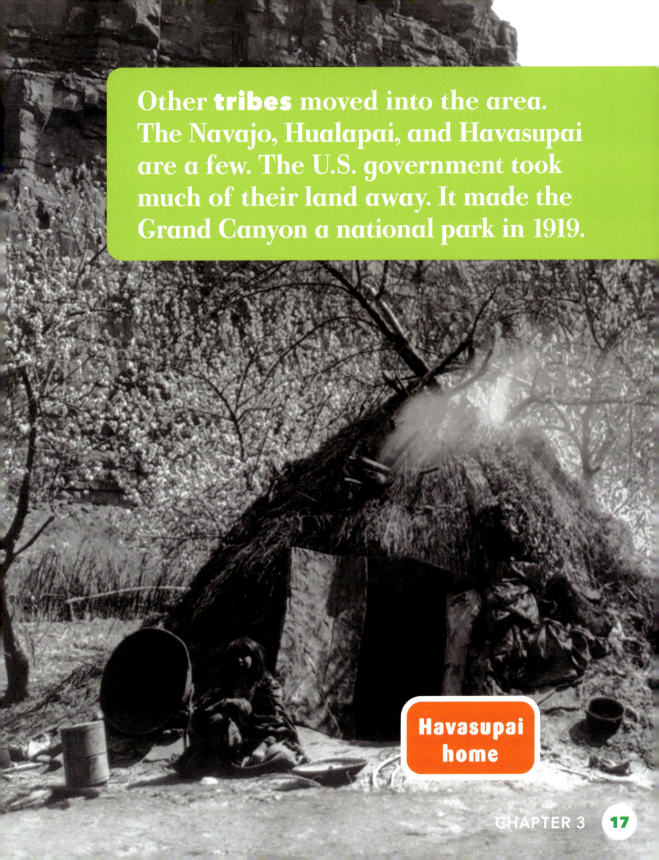

Other **tribes** moved into the area. The Navajo, Hualapai, and Havasupai are a few. The U.S. government took much of their land away. It made the Grand Canyon a national park in 1919.

Havasupai home

CHAPTER 3 17

About 5 million people visit each year! Many come to hike along the canyon's **rim**. Others travel to the bottom of the canyon. Some camp. Others ride mules. You can also take a raft on the river!

DID YOU KNOW?

The Grand Canyon can be dangerous. How? The canyon is very steep. It is icy in winter. It is very hot in summer. Hiking can be very hard. It is important to listen to park staff!

18 CHAPTER 3

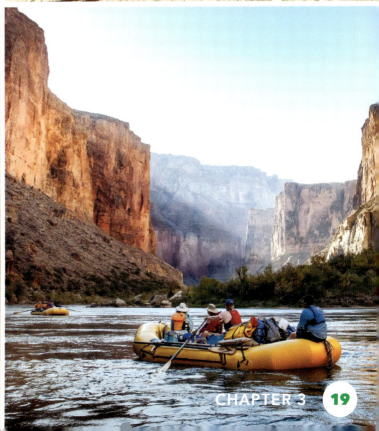

CHAPTER 3 19